A Cup of Poems for the Pain

Fabiola Cherubin

BookLeaf Publishing

India | USA | UK

Presentation by *BookLeaf Publishing*

Web: www.bookleafpub.com

E-mail: info@bookleafpub.com

ISBN: 9789363302594

First edition 2024

I dedicate this book to my beautiful babies, my God you guys are such beauties. This is for you guys! my heart beats for you all! Dreams do come true.

My bombshell best friend Tia, honeyyyyy! you are gold, GOLDEN! God bless me with you 18 years ago. You've stayed on this rollercoaster ride for so long, we burfed on this ride so many times together and you're still here, I owe it all to you. I love you beyond words. You are the epitome of a great sister, person, mother and wife. I, thank you, Tia.

ACKNOWLEDGEMENT

Special thank you to all those who have encouraged me and inspired these poems. I personally wouldn't have made it thus far without you all on this journey.

Thank you to my teachers at John Bowne High School

Thank you Mr. Remeika! you bared with me through my senior year and I never got a chance to properly thank you! To extend the gratitude you deserve, I love you! you do not know how desperately I needed your patience during that time, I was enduring a lot as a teen, all four years of high school. I think you sensed that because of the way you helped push me to graduate. Please, excuse the punctuation. I haven't been in school for a little while. lol I remember that is one of your pet peeves.

To my wonderful English teacher I met in I.S. 8, 8th grade I really dislike the fact I forgot your name. However, your face shines brightly in my head always. I pray God has blessed you tremendously because you do not know how much of an impact you've had made in my life. I read you one poem and you always encouraged me to keep at it, always pouring into my craft during those times, always wanting me to read you a poem. Years later, I realized maybe it was you who pulled some strings to get me in to the Center For Writing program at John Bowne High School. I wish I didn't let life get the best of me and allowed myself to focus more on my academics but home was too loud and I searched for an escape all the time, I should have let my pen take me on a trip instead. I know you'd be so proud to know about this book. I love you, always! may the Universe guide you to this book. I know you'll know this is for you.

Last but not least but to the one who is the head of my life, God, I thank you!!!! MAN! this has been a ride but boy was it worth it, so much thanks. thank you for always being faithful, for your mercy and guidance. I, thank you, Lord.

PREFACE

This book is filled with poems that are relatable! These are truly some tough times we are all enduring; I believe that there is at least one poem in the book that will inspire you. It's important to keep poetry alive, it's therapeutic for the soul.

Changing Scenes

Everything happens in its time
If you sit back and trust
you'll be fine
It's all divine
every phase
Every day
Every lesson
Every blessing
It is all purposeful
If you switch your vibration, the solution will be
clear
you'll realize you have no reason to fear
For no matter what it may look like your season
is near

Line to the Divine Pt.1

A few words I've been wanting to get off of my
chest
Most high, I know that I haven't been on this line
in awhile
I know you hear me because you are within me
but I ask, can I be closer to thee?

Line to the Divine Pt. 2

Can I be closer to thee?
Help me to take heed to the signs the Universe
sends my way
At times my aura is gray
Lord, when it gets like this
please lead me to your gateway
For a private getaway
just for a few days
So I may gain some wisdom
a bit of insight
I know your answering machine is filled up
I won't leave a message
Instead I began searching
Along the way I stumbled upon you
You said, "Daughter, I was with you while you
were contemplated
leaving the message on my line. You couldn't
sense my presence because you weren't vibrating
high and intoxicated with the spirit of wine"
I fell into your arms as I sober like a child
I fell into you and its here I will forever lay

Coming Out of It

You know how the saying goes,
"There's plenty of fish in the sea"
In my world, you were my fish and my fish
only!
In reality you made yourself available for
everybody but me
At my lowest I needed you
you neglected me
You claimed you loved me but treated me as if
you hated me
I crossed the ocean to save you while you
allowed me to drown
when my hand was stretched out
Luckily for me I am rougher than the current
I laid in the sand as the sun revived my lifeless
body
I arose with my vision no longer foggy
Did I have SOS written in the sand?!
why are these tainted souls trying to recuse me?
Feels like they want to persuade me
as if I haven't shown that I can stand on my own
I guess you can say the betrayal rearranged me
you cannot get past me
Like high beams on, the truth is blinding
nothing gets past me

I am a Pisces
on top of that, God's hands are upon me
How could you possibly beat that?!

Rollercoaster of Emotions

I've been feeling emotions
I've been here but a bit reserved
I've been searching for me
I am at odds with which places I should look
I've been gaining clarity but somehow the image
is still blurry
I've been contemplating
I've been out of mind
sometimes I think that's quite fine
I'll make my mind a beautiful place to live
'Cuz none of this shit is real
I'm disgusted by the fake love people project
As much as I try to protect my hearty
the art of being myself fails me
Then I'm back to second guessing
I've been feeling emotions
I've been seeing true colors
They've beaten me down to the ground
Each time I get up, my crown, it glows up

Deep Within

She's poetic
She's sensual
not your typical
You'll take notice of it
become intrigued and want to get next to her
but they tend to fumble the goodness that comes
with this goddess
You cannot approach me with mumble jumble
talk
say it with your chest!
You'd crumble if she snaps her fingers and
dismiss you
you'll start to miss her when you realize
her vibe is one of a kind
Her mind is overflowing with beautiful works
she's not all looks
I promise you she's okay with being lonely
'Cuz she feels like wasted energy is costly
Please, think twice before you try to get to know
her
she doesn't have time to coach ya on how to love
her

Renewal

Through God
the rain washes away my sins
The raindrops on my rooftop clears away the
dark thoughts
The sound of the rain is Mozart to my ears
The gratitude in my heart for the fruits that are
about to bear
Close your eyes
It's about to be the best sleep you've had in days

I Need You

Days turn into weeks
Weeks turn into months
and I'm still numb from the pain
Lord, I know it isn't in vain
I'm unsure how much more of this I can bare
which has me with fear
because these emotions might lead me astray
This armor on my chest is getting heavy
the constant battles are becoming overwhelming
I am yelling at the top of my lungs
Father, save me!
Thank you for paving the way!

Greater Knowing

Finally, it clicked
It feels like God performed a miracle in my life
An ounce of pain used to rest within my heart
like a baby swaddled in a blanket
All the strife has oozed from my pores
I realized it only weakened me
it only allowed me to be my biggest enemy
I found the remedy
it surely strengthened me
I am redeemed
I am free
I am walking in my destiny
I am for sure this isn't a fantasy
it is my reality
They probably wanted to drive me into insanity
however, that wasn't God's plan for me

In My Skin

Light shines within me
I am the light
Bright as the night sky on the fourth of July
I shine
Love flows through me
I'll have you feeling like it's Christmas and you
received the gift you wanted
I am filled with compassion and nurture
but please I beg, don't mistake me for your
momma
You can try to bend and break me
I will not fold
I am pleasant but do not try me
I'll become '09 Kanye at the VMA bold

Come

Come be my peace
Wrap me in you
be my fleece
Come breathe my air
Let me blow your mind with beautiful wonders
Come and be open to healthy loving
I promise I'll change your life in a positive way
Come gaze into these eyes
 I'll show you brighter days
Come open minded
I'll fill you with wisdom
Come with pure intentions
we'll create a harmonious love
The melodious frequency this union plays will
forever fill the atmosphere

What I Imagine It'll Be Like

Looking into your eyes is like watching the
sunset
It's just you and I
no need for the latest reality show when I have
my personal comedian next to me
Our laughter sounds like music as it fills the
room
We're intertwined like a snake with its prey
please do not let it end
Lord, this is my only prayer
If I could love myself from the outside
I'd like to imagine this is what it would be like
We start to paint pictures with our words
with our words we painted our own world
Is this what it feels like when love gives you
wings to fly?

Joy

Oh, sweet joy
I think that should be your name
your humor is my saving grace
My soul sings for more of your loving
You are heaven sent
You are my angel
My joy sweet joy
A never ending love story is what this will be
I prayed for joy and here you are
In the past they misused my joy
treated "it" like a toy
They misunderstood my joy
They silenced my joy and closed captioned their
own words
they poked until they received a reaction that
fitted their script
If only they would've looked deeper
they would've seen my joy was hurting
Have no fear joy
I am equipped
you knew it from the moment we clicked
Now come get addicted to this sweet love I have
to give

The Feels

With you I feel so free
this feels like a dream
It feels like it's you I've been trying to reach
through these poems
I'm always left in admiration of the way you
carry yourself
Dang, this is giving me the feels
Baby, I'm on your heels
I'm not ashamed about it because I like what I
see
It's not the physicality
Let me create a few scenes to show you how it'd
be
allow me to put your mind at ease
I promise it's safe to indulge in me
I'm as good as key limes
I should be your main squeeze
If you're feeling what I'm saying
Baby, you have the feels
So, why are you playing?!
Don't cheat yourself
us together would be a treat

Your Chauffeur Awaits Goddess

I'm strutting down like these sidewalks is my
personal runway
The price no longer phases me because financial
freedom is mine
I ain't greedy either everyone will eat but not
everybody has a seat at my table
I've heard so many tales of situations turning
into fables
people turn into animals, vultures
Get too close now they want to start comparing
This is my destiny so I ain't fearing a single soul
On top of that you can smell my anointing
It's potent enough to make a snake choke on its
own venom
I have to keep the momentum going
I'm not doing this to be seen
This isn't for clout
I have mouths to feed
I have earthly angels who cling tightly as they
look up to me
What a joy it is for them to see me rooms we
never thought we'd fill
and it's all due to God's grace, perseverance and
faith

Prophetic Love

I'm intoxicated by your love
you got me addicted to the way you handle my
body
The cat and mouse chase has been a thrill
I don't know if I should chill but at times I climb
myself up the highest hill
I fantasize about all the ways I can make you
happy if you were mine
I think it's quite fine if we took our time to
morph into one
but I'm scared we might become comfortable in
that stage
I believe that you are worthy of the softest,
purest form of love
I would love to leave my mark on your heart and
mind
not in a way that's dark nor possessive
See I like the way that you lead
I'd hold your hand and follow

Recklessly Thinking

Smoke clouds floating in the air as I sit here
Whether it be za or block work
the spliff just doesn't hit the same
No worries I won't try anything further
Maybe a shot of tequila or a glass of wine
Something to help me drift away
Lord knows it won't ease the pain
Some day I feel numb
other days I sense freedom approaching
Am I reaching for something that is out of my
grasp?
It's as if I'm under attack
the way each thought whacks my brain
Still I live with no fear
Armor on I'm gripped up
I'll empty the clip of psalms
then meditate to release these feelings I can't
bear

The Man With The Mask

We're strangers again but this time with painful
memories
This time I'm left to dissect how you deceived
me
I'm playing detective
 trying to find the clues as to how I allowed you
to infiltrate my camp
At night I vamp
My third eye becomes a projector
I play back all the times I allowed you to play in
my face
I watched how you dismantled my space
Forget sticks and stones
 the words spoken by you ignited a rage of fire
within my soul
You burnt me to dust
but like a Phoenix, I must thrive on
This is my rebirth
You'd love to see me in dirt
I simply can't give you the satisfaction for the
fall of my empire
I'm a fighter
I am Divine
I am a queen
I am love

I can't allow anyone to control the way I feel
about myself

9 789363 302594